Carola Riß-Tafilaj

Gypsy Oracle Cards
The Cartomancy Manual

Wort + Ton Verlagshaus

The information, tips and recommendations given in this booklet are meant to be inspirations for the reader and as such they have been carefully considered, checked and tested as thoroughly as possible by the author. Nevertheless, a guarantee cannot be given, nor can anything in this booklet be a substitute for a medical or psychological consultation. The author cannot assume liability for the use or misuse of the information contained herein, nor for personal or material damage or financial losses.

The illustrations are taken from the following deck of cards:
"Gypsy Oracle Cards"
ISBN 978-3-89875-902-1

The permission to use the illustrations from the cards has been granted by the Königsfurt-Urania Publishing House Krummwisch, © Lo Scarabeo, Turin.
www.tarot-online.com

The Deutsche Bibliothek has registered this publication in the Deutsche National Bibliography; detailed bibliographic data can be found in the internet under http://dnb.ddb.de.

© 2013 by Wort + Ton Verlagshaus, 3. edition, www.wort-ton-verlagshaus.com
Producer: Books on Demond GmbH, Norderstedt

All rights reserved; Printed in Germany 2013

Translation: Elisabeth Teutsch

Print: ISBN 978-3-9813645-1-4 | eBook: ISBN 978-3-9813645-5-2

TABLE OF CONTENTS

36 Main Cards and Houses

FOREWORD

Everyone who is interested can learn the art of cartomancy. This manual contains all the information you need.

The "Gypsy Oracle Cards" are a comprehensive deck of cards which enable an in-depth counselling in all areas of life. Despite the historical pictures, the symbolism of these cards is valid and applicable today.

We have deliberately refrained from writing a detailed descriptive text of the cards in this manual; instead, we decided to define symbolism, character, occupation, time and health by means of keywords. The objective of this booklet is to encourage and stimulate the intuition of the user and to function as a long-term reference manual for the professional cartomancer or fortune-teller.

The description of the cards does not claim to be exhaustive, but constitutes a basis that enables the fortune-teller to discover many more explanations and characterizations - unique for everyone.

1 LORD

Symbol
Strength & Reason

Type
Person Card
Client/Inquirer, male
No age specification
positive

Key Words
Willpower, idea, impulse, assertiveness, energy, tradition, protection, aggression, perseverance, sincerity, determination, identity, vitality, companionship

Characteristics
Steadfast, proactive, forceful, confident, energetic, open, self-assured, esteemed, original, creative, courageous, proud, vigorous, elegant, victorious

Above client - his thoughts
Below client - what he is or has
In front of client - what is important to him
Behind client - what he is not interested in

Occupational House
Occupations where strength and stamina are important; stable position in the job

Occupations
Masculine occupations that require strength, determination and ideas

Time   none

Health
Male sexual organs, e.g. prostate gland

2 WIFE

Symbol
Sensitivity & Values

Type
Person and Child Card (6 to 10 years old)
Client/Inquirer, female
No age specification
positive

Key Words
Emotion, empathy, tact, good conduct, cooperation, loyalty, decency,
propriety, morals, ethics

Characteristics
Gracious, charming, sensitive, accommodating, flexible, polite, helpful,
pragmatic, understanding, gentle, careful, maternal, conciliatory, prudent,
having foresight

Above client - her thoughts
Below client - what she is or has
In front of client - what is important to her
Behind client - what she is not interested in

Occupational House
Occupations where accuracy, sensitivity, dexterity, education and foresight
are important.

Occupations
EDP, computer and IT jobs, clockmaker, goldsmith, surgeon, teacher

Time   none

Health
Female sexual organs, e.g. womb, ovaries

3 WEDDING

Symbol
Commitment & Responsibility

Type
Theme Card Love/Partnership

positive

Key Words
Marriage, cohabitation, love, business connections, commitment to work, contractual obligation, promise, loyalty

Characteristics
Bound to something, ready for commitment, bonding, obligatory, honest, charismatic, energetic, vigorous, lively, loyal, a feeling of belonging

Above client - is thinking about partnership/wedding
Below client - has a partnership, feels connected
In front of client - partnership is important to client
Behind client - not interested in partnership

Occupational House
Family business, total dedication to job or career

Occupations
Family therapist, housekeeper, butler, gardener

Time   5 to 7 years

Health
Heart, cardiovascular system, blood circulation, blood pressure, cardiac rhythm, life energy

4 REUNION

Symbol
Assembly & Communication

Type
Object Card

positive

Key Words
Verbal communication, encounter, date, rendezvous, company, contacts, participation, opportunity, meetings, party, invitation

Characteristics
Communicative, open, sociable, gregarious, friendly, sexy, humorous, gay, superficial

Above client - is thinking about making an arrangement
Below client - has arranged a meeting
In front of client - expects a meeting
Behind client - not interested in communication

Occupational House
Meeting, job review or staff appraisal interview, open discussion, agreement

Occupations
Jobs requiring communication and entertainment: lecturer, consultant, university teacher, DJ, actor, politician, switchboard operator, salesperson

Time spring, 14 days

Health
Neck, larynx, tonsils, throat, vocal cords; also speech defects

5 WIDOWER

Symbol
Competence & Experience

Type
Person Card
Father, brother, uncle, father-in-law
40 years of age and over
positive

Key Words
Experience, warmth, good-natured, strength, father figure, trust, dominance, patience, security, love and caring, aplomb, confidence, mastery, independence, authority

Characteristics
Protective, patient, experienced, mature, good-natured, seems older, reliable, impressive, serene, dignified, caring, qualified, competent

Above client - is thinking about father
Below client - is a father, seems older
In front of client - something to do with an older man …
Behind client - not interested in an older person

Occupational House
Older colleague, boss, supervisor, customer; being too good-natured in the work place

Occupations
Requiring a wealth of experience, knowledge and skills, e. g. engineering, special construction; mentor, coach

Time   winter

Health
Skin and hair, allergy, psoriasis, dry skin, acne, boils

6 OLD WOMAN

Symbol
Intuition & Wisdom

Type
Person Card
Mother, sister, aunt, mother-in-law
40 years of age and over
positive

Key Words
Understanding, compassion, beauty, aesthetics, conviction, intelligence, attentiveness, clairvoyance, competence, emotions

Characteristics
Loving, affectionate, self-confident, aware, authentic, courageous, truthful, wise, considerate, prudent, able to defend oneself, clear, intuitive, emotional, sensitive, experienced

Above client - is thinking about mother
Below client - is intuitive and acts on her feelings
In front of client - something to do with an older woman
Behind client - not interested in an older woman

Occupational House
Older female colleague, supervisor, boss, or customer; sensitive and intuitive occupations or activities

Occupations
Inspirational, creative and intuitive work where clairvoyance and experience is important; life counselling

Time   28 days, moon phases

Health
Knee, meniscus, thigh

7 LETTER

Symbol
News & Information

Type
Theme Card

positive

Key Words
Communication (non-verbal), written invitation, fax, internet, e-mail, advertisement, contract, document, information, books, magazines

Characteristics
Communicative, mediating, sociable, eloquent, expressive, poetic

Above client - is thinking about some news or a document
Below client - is outgoing
In front of client - news coming soon
Behind client - not interested in communication or contacts

Occupational House
Offers, applications, business messages, business invitations or documents

Occupations
Jobs to do with language, written & spoken, author, editor, secretary, journalist, the media industry

Time   within 7 days

Health
Sick report, sick call, diagnosis

8 FALSENESS

Symbol
Subconsciousness & Alertness

Type
Animal and Theme Card

negative

Key Words
Something is going wrong, lies, deceit, resentment, jealousy, betrayal, secrecy, excuses, extra-marital affair, envy, flattery; attention, freedom,

Characteristics
Cautious, shrewd, shifty, crafty, wide-awake, intelligent, egotistic, distrustful, mysterious, obscure, freedom-loving, individualistic sanctimonious

Above client - is thinking deceitfully about someone/something
Below client - is jealous or not honest
In front of client - a mistake will occur soon
Behind client - believes in the truth

Occupational House
Wrong job, bad shop morale, envious co-worker; wrong plan, undertaking or company, wrong attitude

Occupations
Seeking the truth; prosecuting attorney, lawyer, detective; illegal business

Time   wrong timing; nocturnal

Health
Undefinable illness or hypochondria, wrong or uncertain diagnosis

15

9 CONSOLATION

Symbol
Change & New Start

Type
Theme Card
Distance Card: up to 100 km

positive

Key Words
Moving house, act of providence, transformation, change, a new start, nervousness, protection, victory, alteration, development, reversal; **left:** stagnation, **right:** growth

Characteristics
Fickle, erratic, capricious, flexible, progressive, proactive, agile, bold, ambitious

Above client - thinks about change
Below client - is capricious/flexible
In front of client - change is coming soon
Behind client - not interested in change

Occupational House
Change of job, change within the company, company moves location, reorganization

Occupations
Jobs with variety and requiring flexibility, changing tasks

Time unpredictable, faster than was expected

Health
Musculoskeletal system, hip, joints

10 JOURNEY

Symbol
Travel & Vehicle

Type
Animal and Theme Card
Distance Card: up to 50 km

positive

Key Words
All vehicles, car, truck, motorcycle, tractor, airplane; movement, enterprises, tour, adventure, dynamics, noble-mindedness

Characteristics
Agile, athletic, active, vivacious, going forward or making progress, adventurous, fast, impulsive, persevering

Above client - can't relax
Below client - is very agile/temperamental/athletic
In front of client - sth. is making progress during the next weeks
Behind client - things will calm down

Occupational House
Job requiring business travel, business trip, being away on duty, being on the road a lot; a project or enterprise is gaining momentum

Occupations
Truck driver, taxi driver, bus driver, mechanic, construction worker, pilot, courier/messenger service, sales representative, transportation industry

Time   10 days

Health
Motor functions of the whole body, muscles

11 SURPRISE

Symbol
Riches & Prestige

Type

Theme Card Money

positive

Key Words
Wealth, superabundance, material values, luxury, manifestation, profit
left: there is a lot of money to pay; **right:** great amount of money coming

Characteristics
Materialistic, cannot let go, hard-hearted, clinging, proprietorial, possessive, speculative, inheritance, greedy, lucrative, useless

Above client - thinks about property, possessions, money
Below client - has a materialistic attitude, clings to possessions
In front of client - will receive money, property is very important
Behind client - prestige and material values are not important

Occupational House
Well-paid work; holding on to the job under all circumstances, collector's passion

Occupations
Jobs having to do with finances; stockbroker, speculator, shareholder, investor, business man/woman, tax consultant, having independent means

Time up to 5 years

Health
Accumulation of water in the body

12 YOUNG WOMAN

Symbol
Wishes & Contentment

Type
Child Card
Daughter, sister, granddaughter
age: 10 to 19 years
positive

Key Words
Well-being, being in love, lightheartedness, life-style, creativity, youth, beauty, emotion, spiritual wealth, visions, gratitude, pleasure

Characteristics
Creative, emotional, charming, amiable, likeable, many-faceted, seductive, inventive, sensual, friendly, passionate, easy-going

Above client - thinks about a female person
Below client - is creative and imaginative
In front of client - contentment will come about soon
Behind client - has been very creative and happy recently

Occupational House
Young co-worker or boss (female); job satisfaction

Occupations
Jobs having to do with serving, beauty and well-being; cosmetics, manicure, podiatry, wellness, massage, art

Time   7 to 9 weeks

Health
Breast and mammary gland

13 MONEY

Symbol
Security & Finances

Type
Theme Card Money

positive

Key Words
Bank and banking transactions, checking account, financial investments, shares & stocks, stock exchange, speculations, loan, credit, mortgage, savings account, bank guarantee, letter of credit

Characteristics
Risk taking, thrift, materialism; stability, security and hierarchic structure is very important, conscientious, fastidious

Above client - is thinking about their finances
Below client - always has a nest egg
In front of client - next month, financially, there will be …
Behind client - client had financial difficulties recently

Occupational House
Work is secure and well-paid, works at a finance, insurance or investment institution

Occupations
Connected to bank and stock market: bank clerk, customer consultant or account representative, broker, administrator (caretaker, curator, custodian, steward, speculator, investment banker)

Time   none

Health
Confluences, accumulations, cancer, tumor, myoma, cyst

14 MELANCHOLY

Symbol
Mind & Mental Block

Type
Theme Card

negative

Key Words
Sadness, problems, loss, pain, disappointment, limitation, constraints, delays, frustration, obstacles, inhibition, task, passive, depressive state of mind

Characteristics
Strenuous, rigid, slow, unfeeling, numb, hesitant, alone, hopeless, desperate, weak, phlegmatic, pessimistic

Above client - thoughts running in circles, brooding
Below client - is blocked mentally, emotionally and physically
In front of client - there will soon be stagnation
Behind client - there have recently been stress and pressures

Occupational House
Work is very stressful, business is bad; bullying, problems at work

Occupations
Jobs having to do with people and the mind, psychology, physical therapist, priest, pastoral care

Time delay, 3 to 6 months, autumn

Health
Depression, all psychosomatic illnesses

15 LOVE

Symbol
Love & Eroticism

Type
Theme Card Love

positive

Key Words
Harmony, togetherness, eroticism, relationship, partnership, energy, heart, affection, sexuality, loyalty, sincerity, tenderness

Characteristics
Pulsing, energetic, loving, caring, nurturing, ready for commitment, hearty, generous, faithful, loyal, peaceful, emotional

Above client - is thinking about love and sex
Below client - has a loving attitude
In front of client - love is about to come
Behind client - client was in love recently

Occupational House
Business relation or partnership, joint practice, meeting someone at work, client loves his work

Occupations
Humanitarian jobs having to do with love for people; management, organization, business partnerships, brothel, Tantra massage and prostitution, gynaecology

Time   short, unpredictable; right timing

Health
Venereal diseases, abdomen

16 THOUGHT

Symbol
Plans & Judgement

Type
Theme Card

neutral

Key Words
Ideas, reflection, contemplation, hermit, deliberation, inquiry, judgement, imagination, time, transience, mysticism, education, immortality

Characteristics
Understanding, making plans, cautious, foresighted, prudent, thoughtful, educated, profound, noble, lonely, reserved

Above client - is making plans for ...
Below client - is withdrawn and absent-minded
In front of client - has ideas about ...
Behind client - client has recently made plans

Occupational House
Making plans about the job, working in intellectual and mystical areas

Occupations
Jobs requiring exact planning; engineer, architect, philosopher, professor, doctor

Time 4 to 6 weeks

Health
Headache, pituitary gland, mouth, throat, neck

17 GIFT

Symbol
Joy & Appreciation

Type
Theme Card

positive

Key Words
Adornment, decoration, praise, beauty, dowry, compensation, jewellery, metal, wealth, leadership, command, festive occasion, honor

Characteristics
Ornamental, giving, benevolent, ceremonious, exuberant, cultured, aesthetically minded, even-tempered, burdened, hermetically sealed

Above client - thinks positively
Below client - is temperamental and talented
In front of client - something happy is coming your way
Behind client - the inner happiness has been lost

Occupational House
Professional recognition, promotion

Occupations
Jobs having to do with merchandise; merchant, salesperson, art dealer, antiques dealer, negotiator, retail and wholesale trade, broker

Time   none

Health
Power of self-healing, self-regulating forces

18 CHILD

Symbol
Childhood & New Start

Type
Child Card
Age: 0 to 6 years
positive

Key Words
Birth, childhood, the inner child, trusting, creation, the moment, a new beginning, innocence, simplicity

Characteristics
Carefree, small, uninhibited, thoughtless, zest for life, curious, delicate, creative, sensuous, childlike, naive

Above client - is thinking about a new start or a child
Below client - is creative or naive
In front of client - will make a new start shortly
Behind client - has made a new start

Occupational House
Fresh start, new job, new function within the company

Occupations
Jobs having to do with children up to 5 years of age; midwife, youth welfare officer, pediatrician, pediatric nurse

Time   the present time, instantly

Health
Children's diseases, measles, mumps …

19 DEATH

Symbol
Separation & Transformation

Type
Theme Card

negative

Key Words
Sorrow, divorce, ending, infinity, rebirth, metamorphosis, perception, inheritance, heritage, transition, transcendence, change

Characteristics
Profound, wise, capricious, lethargic, freedom-loving, sad, emotional, cruel, destructive, hopeless, unconsciousness

Above client - is thinking about a separation
Below client - is separating from …
In front of client - is in a separation phase
Behind client - a separation has recently taken place

Occupational House
Consensual termination of employment; voluntary change of job, profession, branch of industry or employer

Occupations
Gravedigger, undertaker, funeral home worker, cemetery worker, reincarnation therapist, scrap dealer

Time   Easter, summer solstice, eternal

Health
Serious, prolonged illness, fainting

20 HOUSE

Symbol
Property & Independence

Type
Theme Card

positive

Key Words
Property, house, real estate, assets, plot of land, ownership, stability, background, ancestry, leadership qualities, family, feeling of security

Characteristics
Stable, structured, fundamental, immobile, attached, bound, committed, practical, existential, materialistic, self-confident, possessive

Above client - thinks about his property
Below client - is stable and restrictive
In front of client - the family is very important
Behind client - withdrawn from the family

Occupational House
Independence, self-reliance, leadership responsibility at work, executive position, management

Occupations
All managerial positions, head of department, team leader, group manager, director, executive board, real estate industry, superintendent, custodian

Time   very long periods, spanning generations

Health
Inherited diseases

21 HOME

Symbol
Privacy & The Home

Type
Theme Card

positive

Key Words
Home, apartment, inner life, interior, family, living space, life style, emotions, inner guidelines, center of one's life, privacy, withdrawal, biological clock

Characteristics
Domestic, phlegmatic, quiet, calm, shy, trustworthy, authentic, rigid, well-being, hesitant, lazy

Above client - thinks about the family
Below client - is a homebody
In front of client - personal life will be important in the near future…
Behind client - home is not important

Occupational House
Home office, working from home, telework, family business, housework, unemployment

Occupations
Cleaning woman, au pair, helping in the family business, furniture store, interior decoration

Time   1 to 31 days

Health
Immune system, infectious disease, e.g. influenza

22 SOLDIER

Symbol
Discipline & Ambition

Type
Child Card
Son, brother, grandson
Age: 10 to 19 years
positive

Key Words
Challenge, mastery, order, rules, endurance, security, stability, companionship, assertiveness

Characteristics
Friendly, cordial, reliable, structured, predictable, persistent, strict, devoted, self-sacrificing, loyal, systematic, limited, hard-working, sporty

Above client - to be set in one's ways
Below client - is disciplined and reliable
In front of client - client will meet a certain person shortly …
Behind client - client looks younger

Occupational House
Colleague, team player, employee, organizer

Occupations
Professions with uniforms, such as doctor, dentist, soldier, policeman, fire fighter, customs official, etc.

Time   18 months

Health
Physician, medical consultation

23 PRIEST

Symbol
Decision & Justice

Type
Theme Card

neutral

Key Words
Orientation, wisdom, honor, clarity, court of justice, inner calling, conviction, belief, philosophy of life, contemplation, search for meaning, harmony, peace

Characteristics
Coming to terms with oneself, regretting, confessing, altruistic, religious, staying true to oneself, self-critical, peaceful, even-tempered, balanced

Above client - is thinking about an existential decision
Below client - is decisive concerning …
In front of client - will make a decision soon …
Behind client - a decision was made recently

Occupational House
Decision concerning job, inner process, business process, court, institution, government agency, the public

Occupations
having to do with government or church authorities, e.g. priest, clergyman, deacon, judge, prosecuting attorney, civil servant

Time   none

Health
Spinal column

24 THIEF

Symbol
Fear & Loss

Type
Theme Card

Negative

Key Words
Streak of bad luck, theft, extramarital affair, violation of the rules, exploitation, danger, burglary, depletion, cowardice, ulterior motives

Characteristics
Fearful, restrained, disrespectful, defenseless, dishonest, dangerous, ruthless, criminal

Above client - is thinking fearfully about imminent losses
Below client - has a fearful attitude
In front of client - will suffer losses shortly
Behind client - losses were limited

Occupational House
Job dissatisfaction, breach of contract; loss of employment,
right: employer terminates contract; **left:** client gives notice

Occupations
Illegal work, dishonest business transactions, charlatan, criminal, destroyer, burglar

Time   sudden, unexpected, unhoped-for; lost time

Health
Operation, medical treatment, vitamin deficiency

25 SCHOLAR

Symbol
Career & Theory

Type
Work Card (intellectual work)

positive

Key Words
University education, success, pension, insurance, promotion, secret, learning process, further education, seminars

Characteristics
Experienced, intelligent, honorable, successful, well-educated, literate, cultivated, distinguished, mysterious, clever, responsible

Above client - thinks about education, success or retirement
Below client - is intelligent and successful
In front of client - success will arrive shortly
Behind client - recently client was successful

Occupational House
Successful at work, career, continuing education within the company, knowledge, retirement

Occupations
The teaching professions, occupations requiring higher education or academic degrees, university and school teachers, lecturer, professor, doctor

Time   none

Health
Spa hotel, rehabilitation, sanatorium

26 FORTUNE

Symbol
Success & Fate

Type
Theme Card
(weakens negative cards by 50 %)

positive

Key Words
Future, fertility, spirituality, act of providence, reprieve, pardon, amnesty, wholeness, salvation, healing, darling of fortune, reconciliation

Characteristics
Capricious, freakish, fate, destiny, being in luck, trusting, relaxed, carefree, optimistic, hopeful, confident, generous, successful

Above client - is thinking about his happiness and his destiny
Below client - feels happy concerning ...
In front of client - an auspicious act of providence
Behind client - has recently had a lucky streak

Occupational House
Happy at work, very positive business transactions, a change for the better, preferential treatment, privileges

Occupations
Jobs in aviation or in the spiritual realm: pilot, reincarnation therapist, healer, shaman, astrologer, numerologist, cartomancer

Time   short, fast, unhoped-for, summer

Health
Alleviates diseases by 50 %, self-healing power

27 MERCHANT

Symbol
Gain & the Unexpected

Type
Finance Card
left: money is to be paid
right: money is paid unexpectedly
positive

Key Words
Refund, small sum of money, insurance, something unhoped-for, trade, commerce, profit, gain, buying and selling

Characteristics
Enterprising, practical, assertive, proactive, joyful, calculating

Above client - is thinking about business/trade
Below client - is enterprising and practical
In front of client - will receive unhoped-for money
Behind client - business is not important

Occupational House
Side job, part-time job, salary raise, sales contract, Master of Business Administration, business economist, sales business

Occupations
All commercial and business occupations, office clerk, administrator, salesperson, retail salesman, wholesaler, secretary, case worker

Time   soon, unexpected, 2 weeks maximum

Health
Eyes

28 WAITING

Symbol
Patience & Life Goal

Type
Time Card

positive

Key Words
Yearning, hope, wishes, expectation, point of time, wanderlust, longing to see the world, general view, foresight, goal, scheme of life, visions

Characteristics
Patient, fearless, prudent, careful, observing from a distance, overview, hesitant, far-sighted, quiet, hesitant, wistful, contemplative

Above client - is thinking impatiently about ...
Below client - is very impatient about ...
In front of client - in about 3 months ...
Behind client - is very impatient

Occupational House
Expectations concerning work, professional aspirations, career goals, looking forward to something

Occupations
All therapeutic professions, all health care work

Time   3 months

Health
Slow recovery

29 PRISON

Symbol
Existence & Exile

Type
Theme Card

negative

Key Words
Government agency, public authority, big building, isolation, inhibition, stagnation, hard and austere times, prejudice, secret, restriction, confinement, limitation, loneliness

Characteristics
Withdrawn, uncommunicative, prejudiced, trapped, imprisoned, near-sighted, inflexible, rigid, sad, lonely, insecure, anxious, inhibited

Above client - has existential fear because of …
Below client - is inhibited and lonely
In front of client - standstill; feeling gloomy about the future
Behind client - hard times come to an end

Occupational House
No professional fulfillment possible - tied too deeply to the present work, workplace or company

Occupations
In a government agency or a big building, e.g. a hotel; also unskilled labor, assistant work

Time   stagnation

Health
Treatment at a health resort, hospital, psychiatric ward, residential care home, nursing home

30 MESSENGER

Symbol
Official Notification & Court of Justice

Type
Theme Card

positive

Key Words
Judgement, clarification, elucidation, hearing, decision, dispute, conflict, justice, announcement, separation, the general public

Characteristics
Contentious, talkative, quick to judge and condemn, judgemental, decisive, able to deal with conflict, being overworked or overwhelmed

Above client - is thinking about a separation from …
Below client - is quarrelsome
In front of client - altercation & conflict will soon arise
Behind client - conflicts have been overcome

Occupational House
Change in employment contract, conflict at work, labor contract, contract notarizations, system of law

Occupations
In connection with the court and the authorities; attorney general, judge, bailiff, notary public, lawyer, juryman or lay judge

Time   10 days

Health
Nervousness and nervous system

31 DOCTOR

Symbol
Stress & Unease

Type
Health Card

negative

Key Words
Discomfort, strain, burdens, something is not going well, recovery, convalescence, problems, short illness, time-out

Characteristics
Sickly, stressed out, feeling unwell, make a pause, rest, sad, weak, nervous, anxious

Above client - thinking causes headache
Below client - is ill
In front of client - in the near future sth. won't turn out as desired
Behind client - stress was overcome

Occupational House
Stress at work, a project is not developing according to plan, work is causing illness, bad working conditions

Occupations
in the public health sector, nutrition counselling, geriatric care and nursing; nurse, doctor

Time   14 days

Health
Ears, stress-caused diseases, sudden hearing loss, loss of balance

32 SORROW

Symbol
Problems & Difficulties

Type
Theme Card

negative

Key Words
Offensiveness, troubles, emergencies, crises, trying to cope, worries, cares, blocks, repressed feelings, unexpressed emotions, failure

Characteristics
Destructive, blocked, intellectual, unfeeling, bottled up, withdrawn, mute, defenceless, hard-hearted, uncommunicative

Above client - is worried
Below client - is blocked and helpless
In front of client - difficulties arise
Behind client - problems were solved

Occupational House
Worries at work, no professional progress, bullying

Occupations
in which problems and crises have to be managed; coach, personnel officer, psychologist

Time   none

Health
Teeth, mouth, throat, jaw, migraine, general infirmity

33 DESPAIR

Symbol
Doubt & Deceit

Type
Theme Card

negative

Key Words
Esteem, reputation, honor, dishonor, fraud, deception, respect, dignity, disgrace, loss of face, shame, fear, sadness, hopelessness; value system

Characteristics
Disgraced, denounced, deceived, debased, raped or defiled, cheated, betrayed, insulted, sad, hopeless, helpless, dejected, discouraged, humiliated, dishonored

Above client - is thinking too much
Below client - feels unworthy/undeserving
In front of client - can't see a way out
Behind client - has overcome his doubts

Occupational House
Something is rotten or corrupt, bullying and deceit at work, stress and heavy workload

Occupations
which reveal secrets, hidden motives and serve justice; detective

Time   unexpected, fast

Health
Gall bladder, liver, spleen, poisoning, burnout, blackout

34 SERVICE

Symbol
Work & Practical Experience

Type
Work Card
(practical/technical/mechanical work)

positive

Key Words
Typically masculine work, employment contract, practical work or trade,
activity, strength, perseverance

Characteristics
Hardworking, diligent, active, subservient, obedient, courteous, obliging,
vigorous, energetic, enterprising, ambitious, persistent

Above client - is thinking about work
Below client - is active and diligent
In front of client - work is very important
Behind client - work and self-fulfillment are not important

Occupational House
Permanent job contract; efficient, hard-working, competent, practical job,
reliable, capable, assertive

Occupations
which require strength, assertiveness and practical skills, having to do with a
trade, e.g. roof thatcher, butcher, gardener, painter, mason, plumber

Time   none

Health
Hands, arms and joints

35 CONSTANCY

Symbol
Life's Journey & Reorientation

Type
Theme and Time Card

positive

Key Words
Phase of life, imperturbability, unchanging values, foundation, goal, a new start, change, permanence, stability

Characteristics
Long-term period, continuity, steadiness, reliability, consistency, solidity, long-lasting, purposeful, determined, patient, far-sighted, prudent

Above client - is considering reorientation
Below client - has a persevering and purposeful attitude
In front of client - will begin a new phase of life
Behind client - a phase of life was finished

Occupational House
A change of profession or field of activity, line of business, trade or industry within 2 years

Occupations
connected with nature: forest ranger, lumber jack, horticulture, landscaping, road construction, biologist

Time   up to 2 years

Health
Protracted disease, no quick cure possible

36 HOPE

Symbol
Longing & Spirituality

Type
Theme Card
Distance Card: 1000 km or more

positive

Key Words
Foreign countries, horizon, illusions, spirituality, emotions, overseas, dreams, ideals, beauty, perfection, addiction

Characteristics
Idealistic, long-lasting, forgetful, absent-mindedness, hopeful, emotional, sensitive, creative, clairvoyant

Above client - is thinking about foreign countries
Below client - has illusions
In front of client - has great hopes
Behind client - is very realistic

Occupational House
Work in connection with people, spirituality, foreign languages

Occupations
in the realm of spirituality, in contact with the spiritual world:
psychic powers, spiritual healer, Reiki, clairvoyant, psychic powers, travelling abroad; interpreter, translator, masseur, aroma therapist

Time   all night to early morning

Health
Gastro-intestinal disease, chronic diseases

PRINCIPAL CARDS
WITH THEIR
NUANCE CARDS

CHILDREN

Symbol
Child
Age: 0 to 5 years

Symbol
Wife

Child Card
Age: 6 to 9 years

Symbol
Young woman
Age: 10 to 19 years

Symbol
Soldier
Age: 10 to 19 years

LOVE & FRIENDSHIP

Symbol
Harmony, peace, partnership,
mediator between the worlds,
messenger of God

37 FAITHFULNESS

Symbol
Circle of friends, friendship with male persons
Animal Card
Trust, loyalty, instinct

38 FRIEND

Symbol
Circle of friends, friendship with female persons
Romance, purity, forgetting, honesty,
order, inner peace

39 SWEETHEART

Symbol
Love & Acquaintances
Person Card: Lover, sister-/daughter-in-law
Age: 20 to about 39 years

40 LOVER

Symbol
Love & Acquaintances
Person Card: Lover, brother-/son-in-law
Age: 20 to about 39 years

FALSENESS

Symbol
Something wrong

41 FOE

Symbol
Female Enemy - rival
Intrigues, deceit, fraud

42 ENEMY

Symbol
Male Enemy - detective
Espionage, circumstantial evidence, distrust

WORK

Symbol
Work & Practical Experience

Work as a tradesman, work requiring strength and perseverance
Occupational House: labor contract

43 SERVANT

Symbol
Work & Service

Work requiring sensitivity and tact
Occupational House: a permanent job

Symbol
Career & Theory

University studies, science, professorship, economy, pension
Occupational House: a permanent job

Symbol
Independence & Executive Positions

Freelance Work
Occupational House: independent work, self-employment

HEALTH

Symbol
Stress & Indisposition
Short illness, unease, retreat

Time
8 to 14 days

44 MALADY

Symbol
Disease
protracted disease, being confined to bed, hospital

Time
2 to 6 weeks

COMMUNICATION

Symbol
Rendezvous & Reunion

2 people meet

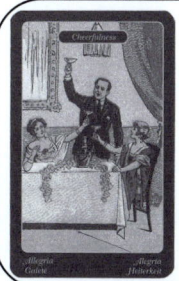

45 CHEERFULNESS

Symbol
Family Celebration & Party

46 CONVERSATION

Symbol
Assembly & Concerts

Dialog, discussion, communication exchange,
circle of friends

47 JOYFULNESS

Symbol
Rituals & Joy

Triumph, success, art, expression,
thankfulness, recovery, gaiety, success

MELANCHOLY

Symbol
Blockade & the Psyche

3 to 6 months

48 SIGHS

Symbol
Emotions & Withdrawal

Short pause to reflect, remember
1 to 3 months

49 MISFORTUNE

Symbol
Aggression & Impetuousness

suddenly, unexpected, unpredictable

CHARACTER

50 HAUGHTINESS

Symbol
Pride & Arrogance

Vanity, longevity, beauty, wealth,
passion, self-love

51 FRIVOLITY

Symbol
Creativity & Tenderness

Rebirth, resurrection, hope,
immortality (souls of the dead)

52 PLEASURE-SEEKERS

Symbol
Gaiety & Exuberance

Friendship, sense of belonging, bonding,
fellowship, support

CARD READING SYSTEMS

THE CELTIC CROSS

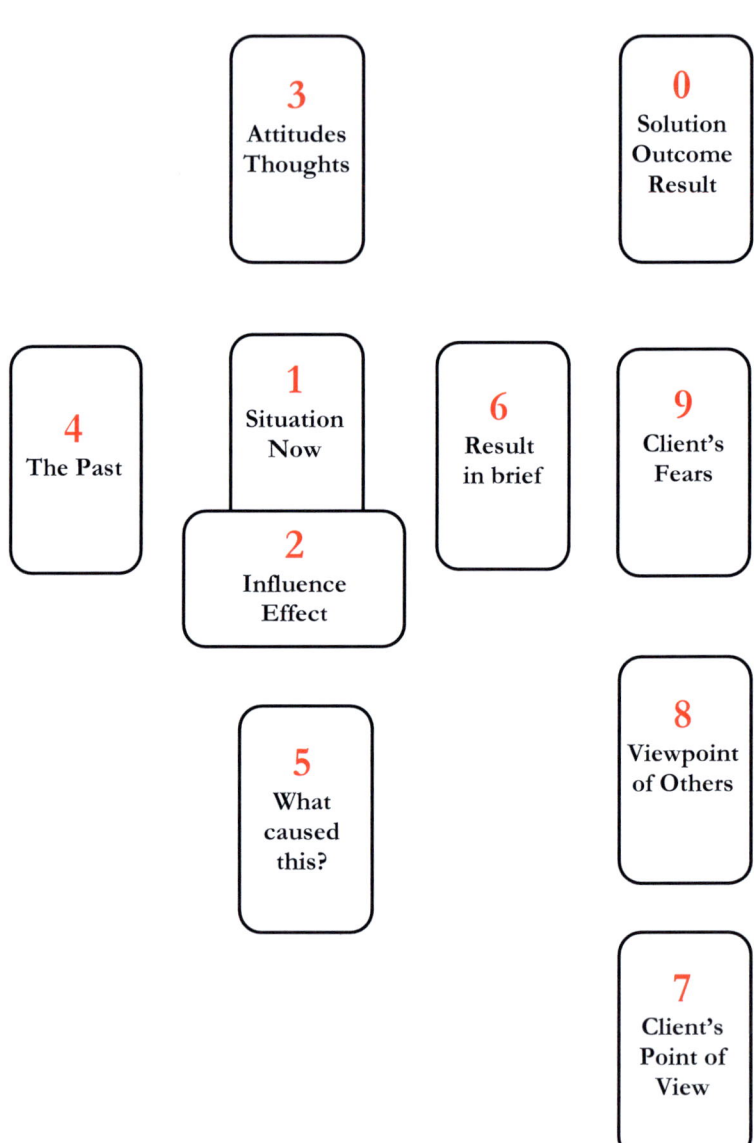

3
Attitudes
Thoughts

0
Solution
Outcome
Result

4
The Past

1
Situation
Now

6
Result
in brief

9
Client's
Fears

2
Influence
Effect

5
What
caused
this?

8
Viewpoint
of Others

7
Client's
Point of
View

THE GYPSY TALON

1. Talon
What affects me directly?

2. Talon
What do I fear?

3. Talon
What helps me?

4. Talon
What lies ahead for me?

5. Talon
What don't I want to accept /what do I refuse to believe ?

THE DECISION

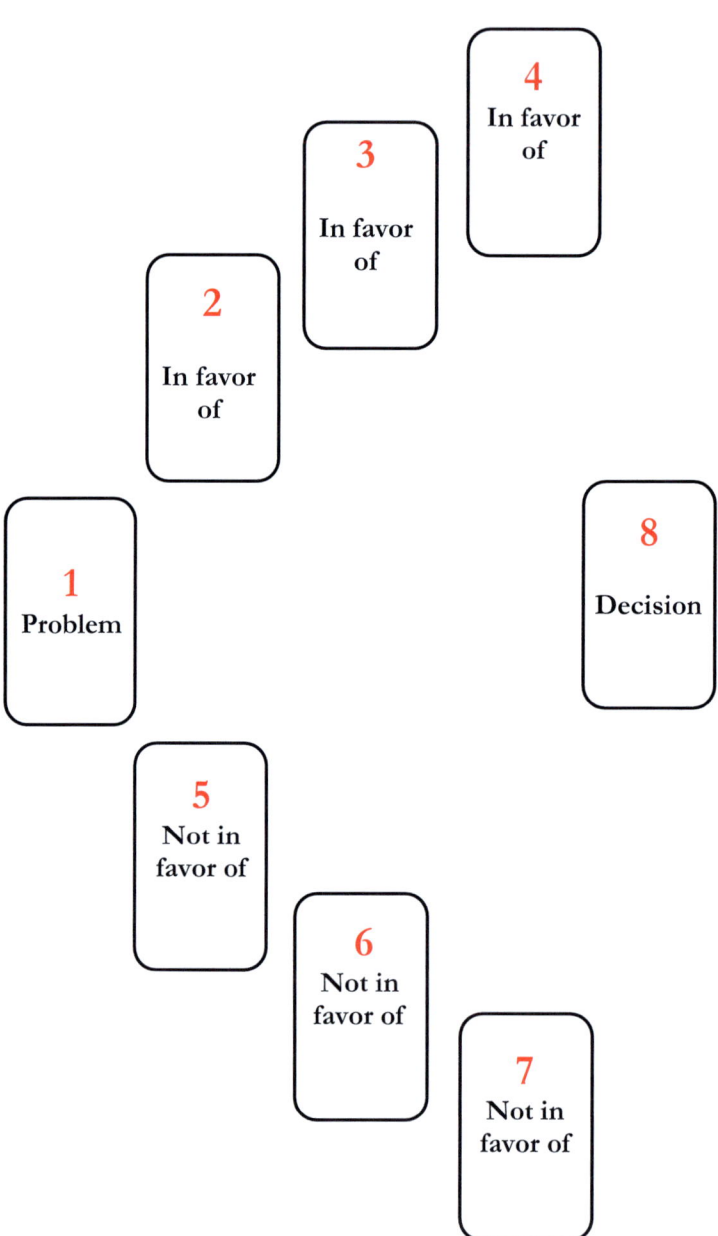

AFTERWORD AND GOLDEN RULES

Spiritual counselling is energy work with a great responsibility. In contrast to holistic psychological counselling or coaching, spiritual counselling is essentially based on the doctrine that there are universal laws of the mind and spirit.

The responsibility of the cartomancer or fortune-teller lies in the trained professional awareness of your intuition and the profound mastery of the tools of the trade, as well as your own positive, exemplary lifestyle. In addition, a cartomancer should be a person who never stops learning new things about the world. The client seeks a confidential atmosphere and needs a sheltered, discreet space, so he can speak freely about everything that is important to him.

Here are my **Golden Rules** for spiritual counselling using the Gypsy Oracle Cards, which I would like to share with you:

- Work with the Gypsy Oracle cards only if you are completely healthy.
- Get attuned to the process of reading the cards
- The first thought that comes to mind is the voice of your intuition.
- The card pattern is a momentary snapshot of the subconsciousness of the client.
- The Spiritual Laws are valid for everyone.
- The solution of the problem lies in the client himself.
- Decisions for a person's life are made by that person.
- Money is energy and a method of spiritual learning.
- Make a note of your card combinations.
- Neutralize the cards after every card reading session.

I wish you every success in your cartomancy work!

Cerdo Zis-Tofilej

FROM OUR CURRENT PROGRAMM

Carola Riss-Tafilaj
Muscle Relaxation after E. Jacobson
Exercises for holistic and deep relaxation
ISBN 978-3-944513-15-7

Deep relaxation also means well-being of the soul. This CD provides easy exercises to learn the technique of progressive muscle relaxation (PMR) to enable you to achieve the fullest relaxation.

Nowadays we so often disregard our yearning and our need for oases of repose and relaxation. And one of the most effective measures to counteract burnout, so widespread a malady today, is deliberate and deep relaxation.

On this CD, the author and speaker Carola Riß-Tafilaj is making a relaxation therapy accessible to the listener, which Edmund Jacobson had already begun to develop at the Harvard University as early as 1908.

Nowadays it is especially important to be able to relax deliberately, in full awareness, in order to be better prepared to cope with the problems of everyday life. With easy exercises to practice this holistic and deep relaxation, the author shows you how to achieve progressive muscle relaxation. The method is to tense a specific muscle group and only then relaxing it. So, by alternating the tension and relaxation, you go through all the muscles of your body, and this will enable you to experience a whole new body awareness in a surprisingly simple and quick way.

Here you can learn to be fully aware of each individual muscle fiber. When body and soul are in harmony, truly great things can be achieved.

The Audio CD "Muscle Relaxation" after E. Jacobson is available in bookstores, as a download and under the label FREQUENZIA.

Text: Carola Riß-Tafilaj | **Speaker:** Steve Taylor
Music: © by Suzanne Teng and Gilbert Levy, www.suzanneteng.com
LABEL: FREQUENZIA MUSIK WORLD, www.frequenzia.biz

KÖNIGSFURT
URANIA

Lenormand

Mystisches Lenormand
Fiechter, Regula Elizabeth /
Trösch, Urban
36 Karten, 57 x 89 mm
ISBN 978-3-03819-041-7

Mystisches Lenormand - Lernkarten
Fiechter, Regula Elizabeth
36 Lernkarten + 11 Anleitungskarten =
47 Karten, 95 x 140 mm
ISBN 978-3-86826-701-3

Lenormand - Blaue Eule
Lenormandkarten mit Karten-
abbildungen
36 Karten, 56 x 87 mm
ISBN 978-3-905017-03-8

Lenormand Orakelkarten mit Versen
36 Karten, 53 x 85 mm
ISBN 978-3-89875-779-9

www.koenigsfurt-urania.com
Wir unterstützen den Ersten Deutschen Tarotverband (Tarot e. V.): www.tarotverband.de